50 shades
of
Feeling Blue

Claire Louot

DEDICATION

This collection of poems is dedicated to Ruksar and Diane for their continued support and love throughout the writing of this book also within my own life; they've helped me in more ways than anyone can imagine.

Claire Louot

CONTENTS

AUTHOR'S NOTES

Writing poetry has been a real creative outlet, not a bolt out of the blue but rather a golden opportunity. Through my rhyming or non rhyming verses I have been able to show my true colours in this anthology of my poetry. Poetry has been a major part of my life either as a reader or as a writer. To name the different sections of this collection, I have chosen variations on the colour blue to stick to my main theme of 'Feeling Blue'. Blue is my favourite colour, it is the colour of the sky and the sea and it is also associated with human feelings and has strong symbolism. Blue can be seen as a soothing colour that is beneficial to the mind and the body.

Sky Blue is the colour of the sky at noon, pure, deep and with no limit but even though the sky might be the place of your dreams or your spiritual feelings it can become clouded and overcast to symbolise sadness or bad things to come.

Ocean Blue is associated with open spaces, freedom and inspiration paired with the vital, natural element of water which represents life and its hardship. The ocean can have daunting widths and depths. It can also be calm but high crashing waves can threaten to drown a person. The ocean stands for emotion and the chaos that follows when sudden obstacles are encountered.

Midnight Blue is a dark shade of blue the sky displays when only lit by the moon, yet it is not the darkest time of the night. Midnight is a dark time not only in a physical way but also in the form of a metaphor relating to a dark time in a person's life. When thoughts creep in at night as you lie on your back and stare at the infinity of the sky suffering is at its height.

Electric Blue is the brightest colour blue. It is so bright it will blind your face with its electrical properties. It makes me think of an electric discharge, hence it is intense and vibrant like a sudden bright spark, a result of dramatic experiences that have rocked my life.

Light Blue is the colour most linked to creativity. But for me even though the light might be the most universal and fundamental symbol, it narrates melancholic episodes that convey coldness and low spirit sometimes bordering irrational thinking.

After this short introduction let us now walk into the Blue.

Blue

Blue is not as passionate as red,

    Not as pale as white,

    Not as aggressive as yellow,

    Not as pathetic as grey,

    Not as depressing as black,

Blue is a peaceful colour

Blue embodies my feelings,

When I'm feeling blue, out of the blue

Then everything turns black

The whole picture becomes a shadow

Light a candle and it comes back

Trapped by a protective halo,

A shiny glow,

If only you blew away the blue

I would be true,

True to my feelings.

1 SKY BLUE

Sky Blue is the colour of the sky at noon, pure, deep and with no limit but even though the sky might be the place of your dreams or your spiritual feelings it can become clouded and overcast to symbolize sadness or bad things to come.

Claire Louot

Spring

The birds on the trees

Singing along

The blossoms

A bird on a leaf

A colour

A flower

A bee on a white flower

A bench

A shadow

The wind

A sound

A murmur

Deliverance

Disappearance

A blank picture

Just lines on a white paper

Cloud

Another day without seeing the sun

It is raining in my heart

The sun has gone on holiday,

The rain has settled inside of me.

I am watching in silence

The nonsense of humanity

I would like to shout :

'I can read your mind'

"Je peux lire vos pensées."

I know what is going to happen,

Isn't it though only a utopia?

Only the day dreamers share my thoughts.

Going far away,

Escaping the emptiness of life,

Sinking into oblivion.

Flying over emptiness and silence

On a cloud which drops rain

On an insipid and grey life,

On unconscious people,

On a silver cloud.

Sunset

I would really like to be alone

Have some time to myself

To stop and ponder.

Let the summer sun

Gently caress my skin,

Lie on some fresh grass

Off the beaten track.

Out there in the wilderness

Just gazing at the traces

Planes leave in the sky,

Give a name to the clouds

Scattered along the path.

As the sun slowly disappears in the horizon

And the sky turns pink,

I close my eyes

And it is darkness again.

Dreams

Close your eyes and you will see

A whole different world coming to life

When everything is dark and quiet

Let your thoughts conduct your mind

Let your mind conduct your dreams

Imagination is a wonderful mechanism

That only humans can operate

Dreams can be colourful and sweet

Or even bizarre and unexplainable

But for me adventures are the expression of dreams

And the worst nightmare is sometimes

When your dreams come true.

I am your Angel

I am your angel because I care for you

I am your angel because I am here for you when you feel hurt

I am your angel because I cheer you up when you are sad

I am your angel because I will always look after you

I am your angel because I take the pain and fear away

I have no wings as I do not need to fly so

It is easier for me to come into your dreams

Just to make sure you are always safe

I am the angel made for you

For you to own

I have not fallen from the sky

I have been sent to show you the path

I am your angel of hope of a better life but

Above all I am the angel of your life because I love you

Claire Louot

In your eyes

I cannot take my eyes off your eyes

I feel drawn into them

So that I just want to drown in them

And simply wish I could stay there for hours

Each time I look into your eyes

I pray I could leave all the troubles

Of the world well behind

As they act as a guide to my life

When I gaze into your precious eyes

They tell me so many things

I can see they have witnessed

Painful memories

And then I myself become lost

In a myriad of memories

If a tear glows in your eye

I feel obliged to wipe it

Because I want you to see the light

As it seems they mirror your soul

And I can almost undress your soul

Through the depth of your eyes.

There is a part of mystery

In your slightly slanted eyes;

Whether soulful or dreamy

Whether open or closed.

They are so pure and limpid

That they simply look like

The eyes of an angel

And they are the door to your heart.

I care

I care for you deeply

I care for your feelings

I care for your needs when I can

I want to be close to you

And you close to me

So you can see how much

I really care for you

For every move you make

Makes me feel alive;

With you around

My world is not cold and dull

I care so much that

When you are hurting

My heart is aching too

I want you to know

That you are not alone

Everything is meaningless

Unless you take care of yourself

And you let me take care of you

Because I care deeply for you

I will…

I might not be family

But you can be sure

I will always bring myself to you

To make sure you are constantly safe

I will give you a blanket

To keep you warm

I will catch a rainbow

To add colours to your life

I will share your hopes and fears

To let your inner confidence grow

I will give you a piece of my heart

To seal our precious trust

I will hold your hand tightly

So you can feel my love

I will share this poem with you

To show you how much I care

Your dream

I can see in you the potential

That one day you will be

What you have always wanted to be

One day you will realise

That you are the person you dreamed of

As you had the potential and the courage

To hold onto your dreams

Against adversity

You need to continue your journey

Towards becoming a truly amazing person

I know fully that if you stumble

You will pick yourself up

And taking one step at a time

You will reach your goals

And you will then see

That your dream has become reality

Claire Louot

What is happening to me?

What is happening to me?

Am I going insane?

Have I found someone to accept me as I am?

Someone who has touched my heart

Someone who can hear me cry inside

Someone who can feel the pain I never show

Someone who wants me to remember the good times

And wipe away the bad ones

From my bruised soul

What is happening to me?

Someone is trying to take away some of the pain

Which I have been fighting against for years

I can feel my heart is slowly opening again

My blood is turning hot

I have found someone I can empty my heart on

I want you to know

I would not be the person I am today

Without you

Through your comforting hugs

I am trying to pull myself together

For you and thanks to you

What is happening to me?

You know I'm shy on the phone

And express myself better in writing

You are the only person I can tell my soul to

I just hope never will you turn

Your back on me

What is happening to me?

No matter how busy I might be

I will always make time for you

I will endeavour my time to soothe your fears

And I will repeat again and again

That I do care for you

And I promise my hugs will be extra special for you

Claire Louot

2 OCEAN BLUE

Ocean Blue is associated with open spaces, freedom and inspiration paired with the vital, natural element of water which represents life and its hardship. The ocean can have daunting widths and depths. It can also be calm but high crashing waves can threaten to drown a person. The ocean stands for emotion and the chaos that follows when sudden obstacles are encountered.

Claire Louot

Grail

Walking towards the light

In quest of the truth

Pausing now and then to think

Fighting against the obstacles

Scattered along the road

Strangely enough,

People,

Nice people

With similar stories

Are encountered on the journey

The light is very near now

But still the question mark is here

Flashbacks destroying the brain

Flashbacks letting you down

Shame, but who is to blame?

Heart, mind and soul

All torn apart,

Open heart operation

And yet the Grail is not

Within reach or eyesight

Light sailing

A special person has been sent my way

And surprisingly, our paths have crossed.

We have now embarked on a journey

Through the rough ocean of life

To sail together with no buoy.

We will brave the tempest

To come ashore to a field of joy.

Let us just hope

That the years will not erase

The priceless gift of our growing friendship

For, to me, you are a gift of God

A true friend I am indebted to

Who has made my world a more beautiful place.

So now,

Do not blow the candle.

Let the flame of our friendship

Brighten our lives

And promise me that no matter how far,

You will not let the flame die.

Going away

If only life could be simple

But reality is different

All I want to do

Is see a different world

Where everybody gets on

Where there is no competition

Where love is all around

But instead, I have to run away

Run away, go away all the time

I am tired of going away

Can't anyone trust me?

See me for what I'm worth?

Stop me from running?

But I'm on my own,

And in order to live and survive,

I have to run away

And live my life on my own

And it seems that at the end of the day,

I just love going away.

Got to find a better place

Why?

Why do I live ?

Why do I die ?

Why do I scream ?

Why do I cry ?

Why do I laugh ?

Why do I talk ?

Why do I see ?

        Why, why?

I watch a leaf falling from a tree

    Flat on the ground, why ?

I watch the sun going down

    Far away on the horizon, why ?

Mother nature is not as cruel

    As human beings are, why ?

Even the echo is not answering me

        Why ?

Why is there just me

    Lost in my deepest thoughts, why ?

Why are you all the same,

        Why ?

Silence

Silence is beautiful

But can be painful

It has haunted my life

And I have enjoyed it

From time to time

Silence is like a hollow cave

Dark, empty, scary

Silence is heavy

Sometimes I would like to grasp it

And at times to sparkle it.

Contrasts

As the sun is rising

A new day is coming to life

I stand there looking

As Eve was looking at Adam

Look at the pain in my eyes

Is the day going to bring change in my life?

Seize the day

Carpe Diem

Profite du moment présent

Thoughts controlling dreams

But the light of day is dazzling me

To take me back to reality

I am scared of the unknown, of darkness

Dust that will turn into dust again

Will you rise again from your ashes?

Life after death

Is life just death postponed?

Where is hope?

My spiritual inspiration

If I honestly ask myself

Who is the person in my life

Who means the most to me

I do not think it is

Someone who has given me advice

Someone who has offered me solutions

But it is

Someone who has touched my wounds

Someone who has shared my pains

With soft hands and warm hugs

Someone who has been by my side

Someone who has stood by me

Through grief

And is helping me heal

Strengthen my soul

And keep my spirits high

No matter if near or far

That precious person

Is my truly spiritual inspiration

Claire Louot

The two sides of my heart

Things happen for a reason

What a common saying

But when people meet

Then experiences are shared

They walk the path of life

Even if it is for a short while

Together hand in hand

A new chapter in their lives

Is being started

Hearts beat fast

To a new-found relationship

Emotions are shared

To keep hearts beating

But my heart is ambivalent

One side has already died

Years, decades ago

This dark side has turned black

Like a petal which has dropped from a rose

That was once young and fit

And has shrunk and wrinkled

Not able to feel anything

The other side regularly bleeds

Letting out little droplets of thin blood

That are reflected on the tears running down my face

That side can still sporadically feel emotions

But has forgotten how to deal with them

Since, when it starts hurting

It feels like a sharp blade slashing

Precise cuts that leave marks,

Visible scars on an organ

Already affected by severe traumas

So half my heart starts beating

For other reasons, probably the wrong reasons

So then all you need to do

Is change two letters in the word heart

To reveal its true meaning

Which then becomes : hUrt

Claire Louot

I know my heart

I know my heart has forgotten

It can beat fast and madly

To passion and even true love

But I know my heart

Has not forgotten

It can slowly and softly feel

The invisible pain

Accumulated over the years

I know my heart

Has been broken

To a myriad of pieces

That will never be

Put back together

I know my heart

Was once made of gold

But with the years

The gold has gradually faded

I know my heart

If only

If only the tears could wash

The pain away

If only water could dilute

My sorrow

If only the news I am hearing

Was not true

If only my broken heart

Could be mended

If only I could hide

My feelings

Would life be even easier?

It surely would

Because with so many ifs

We could build a much better world

Claire Louot

3 MIDNIGHT BLUE

Midnight Blue is a dark shade of blue the sky displays when only lit by the moon, yet it is not the darkest time of the night. Midnight is a dark time not only in a physical way but also in the form of a metaphor relating to a dark time in a person's life. When thoughts creep in at night as you lie on your back and stare at the infinity of the sky suffering is at its height.

Claire Louot

Nocturnal thoughts

I woke up four times last night

Thoughts racing like a speedboat

Thought after thought after thought

Nothing people say can put things right

I think and keep thinking too much

As I remain silent with my eyes shut

Until I feel totally out of touch

Trying to push away the next cut

4 am knows all of my secrets

That moment I burst into tears

The whole night is filled with regrets

Of what look like men marching with spears

As I lay wide awake

There is so much going on in my mind

It is always too much for me to take

Trying to forget about the daily grind

Do not seem to be able to keep my worries aside

Toss and turn swiftly to my side

And all I can do is write things down in my journal

Since my thoughts are nocturnal

Tears

I wish I didn't cry at night,

I wish I didn't cry at all.

Floods of tears digging an abyss

Between my life and the real world

I wish there was a simpler way

To express all these feelings

Imprisoned deep down inside me

I wish I didn't cry at night

Streams of water

Washing away your sins

Tears that make your pain more visible

When there is no fear

Then there is no tear

I wish I didn't cry at night

Claire Louot

When I cry

When I cry

My tears are bitter and cold

They run along my face

Leaving a wet trace

And emotions no one can unfold

I cry when I am alone

Because my heart is broken and torn

I even cry with my friend

And it seems to her there is no end

People think I am in my own world

Floods of tears pour out of my eyes

And nothing can stop the cries

If only you knew what I thought

All the inner battles that I have fought

But this is how I feel

And to me the pain is very real

I am hurting badly inside

So please do not push me aside

I desperately need you now

To help me deal with my sorrow

So when the tears are on their way

Make sure you do not push me away

Just show me your presence

To help me deal with other people's absence

Gone in the blink of an eye

Every minute of the day I think of you

Please someone tell me this is not true

Thinking of you bring tears to my eyes

Because you did not give me a chance to say my goodbyes

So many things I wish I could still say

But now you are just gone so far away

Why is it we had to part

I miss you with all my heart

Even though you are not in sight

I still see your face every night

When I think about how you died

I had to sit down and I cried

Death took you in the blink of an eye

And simply also made me want to die

Now you shine with the stars above

Only because you were carrying so much love

I have a mother, a father and a big brother

The only thing that is missing now is you, my little brother

I cannot wait for God to bring us back together

As I thought we were meant to stay together forever

All I have now is memories to keep me alive

And even to do that I will have to strive

I wish you were still here

Because now nothing seems clear

Claire Louot

Ride In Peace

No matter how hard I try

I still cannot help to wonder why

It had to be you, so dear to my eyes

Of all people who had to so suddenly die

Most times I just can't help breaking down to cry

And it is so hard to move on even when my tears dry

It seems you took the world by storm

From the time you were born

But now in the twinkle of an eye you are gone

I feel so empty I may fail to hang in there all alone

Pierre, dear, you are the one

I will always miss

And now that you are not here to hear this

I will tell you by blowing one more kiss

And praying that God will rest your soul

In eternal peace

Taken from me

I'm sitting here in my room

Looking at your picture

Wondering why you could not be a part of my future

Uncontrollable tears stream down my face

While my heartbeat starts to race.

Asking God why he took you from my life

It was more painful than stabbing me in the heart with a knife

I still needed you here

You were the one to make everything so clear

When you died a part of me died too.

I never knew how hard it was to lose someone you love

Until the day you went to heaven above

Even though I cannot see you

I know you are up there watching over me

I miss you more and more everyday

And all I can do is pray

Claire Louot

Hello sister

There is so much I wish I had said

As I think of you every minute of the day

It still does not seem real you are not around

I keep on saying to myself you will come round

I will never forget the 21st February

While I was at home on a Saturday getting cosy

When the phone went quite late

And the terrible news kept me awake

Surely none of it could have been true

Surely your wife was not talking about you

It could easily have been you on the phone

Saying your favourite English sentence

"Hello sister"

Lying there

I did not want to come

I did not want to see you

Lying there

Your eyes are shut

But yet your mouth is slightly open

You are turning blue

Or is it a bruise I can see

That has been cosmetically hidden

You look cold

Surrounded by five planks of wood

You look ready to go

You are waiting peacefully

For that last plank to seal your fate

Two children's drawings have been placed at your feet

Displaying the message

"Je t'aime papa"

Grief

Grief is inside of me and is not ready to come out

It regularly explodes through unmanageable feelings

Those take over my life at the most inappropriate times

Every move I make has become cumbersome

Every breath I take is weighing me down, almost suffocating me

The utter pain that I feel is a testament to the love I had for you

Uncontrollable pain that leaves small scratches on my body that look like tally marks

A howling wind of sadness is passing through my body

I long for the day when the wind and the dark cloud hovering above

Slowly diminish, very slowly, very gently

Until it is just a sigh and the world becomes a brighter place again

This painful feeling of emptiness

My heart still beats but only just

All my feelings have deserted me

My body seems to be empty

Just an envelope with nothing inside

Looking around even the world appears empty

I do not even want people to approach me

Am I living a nightmare or is this reality?

Will life ever go back to normal?

I cry and scream hysterically inside

But no one hears my painful call

I am sinking into depression

The bottom of despair now seems very accessible

Too many questions left unanswered

Why are my friends talking about my future

When even the present does not seem to hold anything
for me?

How can I cope with tomorrow?

Claire Louot

I am so lost and sick at heart

That I am not able to show any emotion

Only the feeling of dying is bearable

This painful feeling of emptiness

4 ELECTRIC BLUE

Electric Blue is the brightest colour blue. It is so bright it will blind your face with its electrical properties. It makes me think of an electric discharge hence it is intense and vibrant like a sudden bright spark, a result of dramatic experiences that have rocked my life.

Claire Louot

Rage

Rage, a four letter word

R for Reality or Routine,

A Revolt Rumbling, a Rumour

A for Always and Anywhere

Hidden and yet still visible

G for Gross or Great

Two extremes

Paradoxical terms walking hand in hand

E for Envy and Energy

Reveal one and release the other

Rage, a four letter word

To   Release

    A

    Great

    Energy

Broken

When you look at me

What do you really see?

Do you notice the fake smile

Which is only visible for a short while?

If I broke down in front of you

Would you have a clue

As to what to do?

If only you knew

What goes on in that head of mine

Please give me a sign

To show me that you truly care

If only you dare

But hey I'm too complicated

And far from infallible

Am I worth the time?

Am I worth your time?

Do you really want to stand by me

Are you sure you can handle me?

Are you ready to take that risk?

If so, please don't be too brisk

'Cos I'm very broken

Until the truth is spoken

It will take a great deal of courage

To help me carry all this baggage

You tell me you have faith in me

Because you hopelessly want to see me free

Claire Louot

A distorted vision

A little girl is lying in the middle of a field

Where the grass is greener

And the air is purer

She does not pay attention

To the singing of the sparrows

Or the merry-go-round of the rabbits

She looks like a speck of light

In her little white dress

Lost in the immensity of this field

She is gazing at the infinity of the sky

Yet she is unable to see

It is no more than a distorted vision

Through the tears running down her face

It is just another morning

A rude awakening after another sleepless night

Hoping for the new day to bring something bright

I can feel my eyes blotted and red

Just another reason to stay in bed

There is a pile of wet tissues on the floor

No wonder my eyes feel so sore

It is just another morning

I have to get ready for the day ahead

And I already feel totally overwhelmed

I tip over the edge of the bed

Yet another thing which I dread.

Please someone, help me go through today

I really need to push myself and not stop halfway

It is just another morning

Medication is the key to not feeling lousy

Simply hoping it will make me more bouncy

Not stopping in front of the mirror

Else it might be shock, horror

I certainly look like the portrait of despair

As if anybody cares

It is just another morning

My inner battle

I cannot think straight

No matter how long I wait,

I cannot see clearly

Especially when I feel poorly,

I cannot feel anymore

As the battle wounds are now a mental dolour,

I cannot hear what you are saying

Because of the life I have been living.

I cannot smell the fragrance

Of my painful existence

As I am drowning in the shocking realisation

Of my own reflection

Revealing all my true colours

To a world filled with horrors.

I scream inside, gasping for air,

Beneath the mask I always wear

And the pain that I cannot handle

As I know it is truly my own inner battle

Claire Louot

I am hurting inside

The world around me is moving fast

But my world has stopped

The old me has disappeared

As I now live in a solitary retreat

I will continue to sit in silence

Just me and my emptiness

Because no one can see how I feel inside

All I seem able to do is drop one tear after another

And as more tears come, I fall more and more into depression

I do not have the courage to carry on

Since my strengths have deserted me

I do not wish to fight anymore

And simply give in to darkness

As depression is what it brings

I battle with myself though

But I always lose the fight

If only you knew what I thought

If only you knew what I fought

The past did happen

The future might never come

And now the present does not even seem real

Yet I am hurting and the pain in me is very real

Depression has reached my soul

I wish it could go away

Because it hits hard and harder every day

I am unable to engage in a conversation

As I feel my mind has been violated

My whole body is a black hole

All filled with an array of depressing feelings

Since I have lost control

Because I am hurting inside

I have lost control

I have lost control of myself

I do not want to be surrounded by people anymore

Because I do not know what to say anymore

I am sorry I cannot look happy as you would want me to be

I like to hide, away from the world

Seems easier than facing the repetitive questioning

Still thoughts are constantly occupying my mind

The person I loved is now gone

My emotions are totally uncontrollable

One minute I can be happy and the next utterly sad

My heart is bruised so badly

That it seems as if I was standing in a quick sand

Gradually sinking and now

I can cherish the thought of going and not coming back

Hanging on the fragile hope of an unthinkable future

I am losing control as I cannot stop crying

I feel helpless, useless and emotionless

My feelings have now been buried

I am losing power over the things I would like to do

I want to end this journey of sorrow and ease the pain

I feel I have lost control of my soul turned to ashes

My weakness defines the day

I have lost control

I am not in control anymore

I am afraid of my own feelings

I just feel so small, so useless

That I cannot even stand people saying my name

If people look at me

I simply feel too exposed

I try hard to hide the way I feel

And even my true friends cannot understand me

I have to admit defeat

Now that everything has been thrown away

I never thought I would fall down to my knees

All is pain, tears and sorrow

Everything has brought me to crying endlessly

I am still hoping it was not true

I simply want to disappear behind every tear I shed

With my fingers crossed wishing you were here again

But I am left bending and waiting in agony

Claire Louot

My body has now become so cold

Because death lingers

The sun has stopped shining

To leave room for the storm

Which I am watching through the window

And with the storm, things have come to an end

As my weakness surely defines the day

Since you have left, my heart has been weak

I feel so needy and dependent

The scars of my own sorrows stay anchored

And just remind me of my own weakness

I have become numb

Whatever anyone says

My strengths have deserted me

When I have realised

That it is over now

Pain

Why do you always come

Unexpectedly in my sleep

And wake me?

When you know truly

You have not been invited

And you are not welcome!

I have to toss and turn

And in the end simply

Give up.

And bend double

Under the sheer intensity;

And cuddle up

In a foetus shape;

And let me succumb

To the atrocity of the pain

And just become

A baby again

Lost for words

One day I will wake up beyond the perfect cloud

Where I can scream out loud miles away from the crowd

Far from the demons that have been haunting me

And who have stolen and destroyed my inner beauty

I am but lost for words

One day I will push away the trauma

That has given me so much drama

The loss of innocence that was not meant to be

And eventually I shall be set totally free

I am but lost for words

One day I will throw the anchor

That has moored me like shackles tied to a stranger

The callous laughter will stop buzzing in my ear

And finally it will all become clear

I am but lost for words

One day I will be able to stop living and reliving the event

That has given me panic for too many years

Shaped me beyond words until this very moment

And permanently wipe off all the tears

I am but lost for words

Claire Louot

Your world of lies

It goes without saying

That you have a mind of your own

And that you know fully

The difference between right and wrong.

You are now part of my world

And that is the reason why

I can read between the lines

And see the signs;

When you feed me with lies,

You keep me away from the truth

That you store inside

And simply hide

Behind a mask of lies.

At times, I do not know what to believe

Since I do not know what is truth or lie

I want to know what it is that you feel

I want to know the You that is real.

Why do you hide behind your fears?

Are you afraid I won't like you?

Well then, do not say it, if it's not true

'Cos for me lies hurt more than the truth

It seems you act two-faced

Hiding your emotions

To simply go with the motion

Feelings safely locked in

You probably say to yourself,

"A little lie will get through the day."

But as time goes by,

It might turn into bigger lies

With every word you say

And become part of your life

Where underneath truly lies sadness

In your own world,

Your world of lies

Claire Louot

5 LIGHT BLUE

Light Blue is the colour most linked to creativity. But for me even though the light might be the most universal and fundamental symbol it narrates melancholic episodes that convey coldness and low spirit sometimes bordering irrational thinking.

Claire Louot

Words

Words surely are an impure medium

For those born under a bad star,

Some might see amazing combinations

That do not necessarily make sense

Still words can hurt and even destroy.

Words do not come easily

When you want to express your true feelings

To your closest friends.

Words of love never sound right

Even though your heart, mind and soul

Are filled with them;

They have to be uttered to the right person.

Words are simply better sung.

All alone

A nightmare in my dreams

I am feeling sick

To be here, there or anywhere

What is the difference?

Alone,

Alone amongst everybody

Alone in the middle of the crowd

Alone on the earth

Alone in the universe

I wake up on an island

All alone, marooned in the middle of the ocean.

Then my dream is coming to life

Everything stops around me

And stress is tolling the bell.

The sun is stroking my hair

And is shining brightly.

I am boiling

I wake up with a jump;

Alone,

All alone in the dark.

Why me?

It happened one day

When I was not expecting it

And life has drifted away

As I was losing my own identity

Acting as if nothing had happened

And living or surviving

Trying to understand

What I have done

To deserve that?

Was it my destiny

Or just fate?

My life destroyed forever

Memories that cannot be buried

A scar which is not healing

A pain moving you to pity

And me!

Yes, why me?

Claire Louot

Echo

Look at me

Look at my body

The scars are not all visible

My body is hollow

If you touch it

It echoes emptiness

It is a dull sound you hear

That hurts your ears

But my mind is active

Never at rest

Always busy

Words, pictures flashing in my head

And that cannot come to life through my mouth

What you hear is just

The echo of an empty body.

The mirror

Who are you?

Yes, YOU standing here,

Why are you staring at me?

Your gaze is so fierce

It hurts me so much,

That I can almost feel your pain.

You are so empty

Nobody can see you

But can only see through you

And not see what you are worth

But are you worth anything anyway?

I say I can almost feel your pain

But even your feelings are invisible

And even when you look at me in the mirror

It is merely a reflection on you

As you can't see anything

And nobody can see you

Claire Louot

The art of camouflage

I feel like a chameleon

Who has mastered the art of camouflage

As fragile as a dandelion

Under a gust of wind.

Hidden feelings blended in a collage

Emotions tightly pinned

Meandering in my mind in sporadic episodes

Through what seems like antipodes.

A voice only I can hear

That has fallen on a dead ear.

Don't try to understand

What you don't know

Else you might fall in a quicksand

And drown in my sorrow.

There is no point

There are some things

I will never understand

Why do you ask how I am?

And you walk away

When I start answering 'cos

There is no point

Why did you say

You would be here for me

When you know fully

You were too damned busy, so

There is no point

You told me I would always come first

Was it first on the list of people

Who you would forget quickly

There is no point

Claire Louot

Secret friendship

I feel a strange love filling my heart

Not for you or myself

But for the secret friendship we have

I love you like the sister I lost

You do mean the world to me

And if we were to part

It would only leave me with half a heart

No one will ever understand

The friendship we have

Invisible bonds as you call it

But I want you to know

Though far away,

In my heart you are always near

Thank you my friend

You smile when you see me

You make me talk

You have given me an ear

To listen to my ups and downs

Thank you my friend

The talks we have really mean the world to me

You now stand by me when

All my other friends have left

To have found someone like you

Is hard to believe

Thank you my friend

I have put my problems

Into your warm palms

Confessing and opening my heart

Admitting with no lies

You have wiped my tears

As I was holding onto you

Thank you my friend

Claire Louot

I open my heart to you

And you try to mend the cracks

Your gaze still leaves me shaking

Because we are both victims of past dramas

Beyond our own understanding

Thinking of your pain and mine

Hand in hand

In an insipid world where

We seemed to be cursed with darkness

Thank you my friend

You know you can use my shoulder as a pillow

You do not walk in front of me or behind me

But by my side as you are

My right arm

While you are still living in a world of pain

I will protect you and guide you through

As you need a better today

And dream of an even better future

Thank you my friend

That's who I am

The battle with depression that I cannot win

Has led me to become a failure

Yes, that's who I am

The sad look on my face that most people do not see

Has led me to look very ugly

Yes, that's who I am

Thinking of the tears shed on my pillow every morning

Has led me to feel useless

Yes, that's who I am

Even giving all I can to try

Has led me to think I'm going to lose

Yes, that's who I am

Fighting all the thoughts I cannot seem to push aside

Has led me to know I'm not in control

Yes, that's who I am

Claire Louot

My notebook open, musing all alone

Has led me to realise I'm not good enough

Yes, that's who I am

50 shades of Feeling Blue

Claire Louot

INDEX OF TITLES

Claire Louot

50 shades of Feeling Blue

Claire Louot

ABOUT THE AUTHOR

Claire is a language teacher in a secondary school in East London. Born and raised in France she now lives and works in London with her daughter, a student she adopted. In 2013, she received the Jack Petchey Leader Award for outstanding services to education.

She fell in love with the English language at a young age and learnt it at school and University. She graduated with an MA in English Language and Literature in 1994. She developed her passion for writing and photography when she worked as a freelance photo journalist for a French newspaper.

Claire Louot

24950704R00061

Printed in Poland
by Amazon Fulfillment
Poland Sp. z o.o., Wrocław